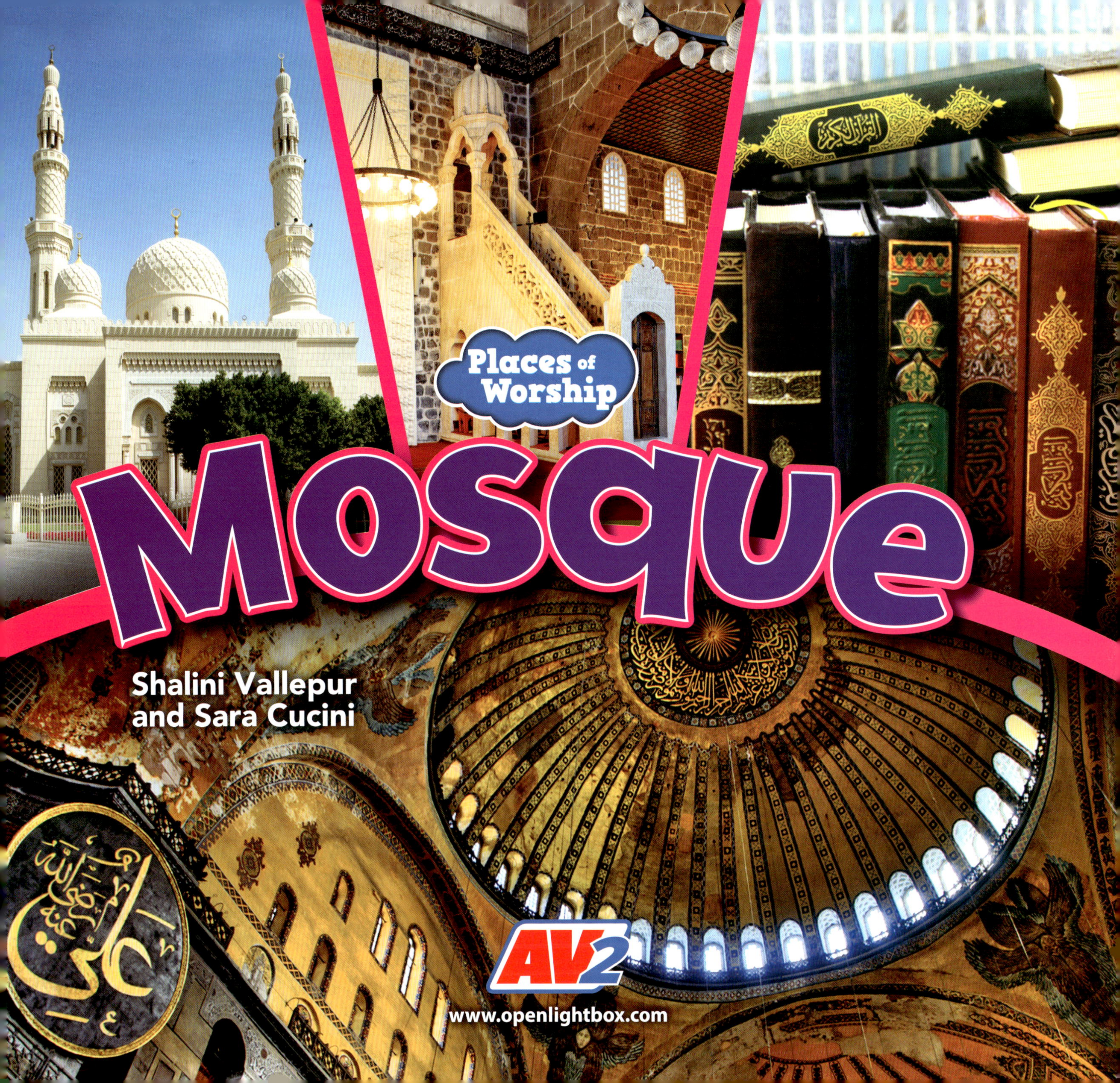
Places of Worship
Mosque
Shalini Vallepur
and Sara Cucini
AV2
www.openlightbox.com

Step 1
Go to **www.openlightbox.com**

Step 2
Enter this unique code
VQPXYUWFE

Step 3
Explore your interactive eBook!

Places of Worship
AV2
Mosque
Start!
Share

Your interactive eBook comes with...

AV2 is optimized for use on any device

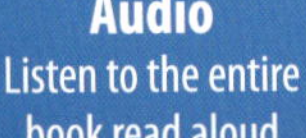
Audio
Listen to the entire book read aloud

Videos
Watch informative video clips

Weblinks
Gain additional information for research

Try This!
Complete activities and hands-on experiments

Key Words
Study vocabulary, and complete a matching word activity

Quizzes
Test your knowledge

Slideshows
View images and captions

Share
Share titles within your Learning Management System (LMS) or Library Circulation System

Citation
Create bibliographical references following APA, CMOS, and MLA styles

This title is part of our AV2 digital subscription

1-Year K–5 Subscription
ISBN 978-1-7911-3320-7

Access hundreds of AV2 titles with our digital subscription.
Sign up for a FREE trial at **www.openlightbox.com/trial**

The digital components of this book are guaranteed to stay active for at least five years from the date of publication.

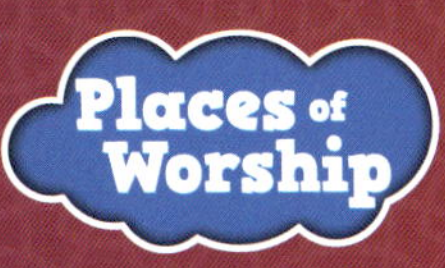

Mosque

CONTENTS

Have you ever been to a mosque? A mosque is a building of worship for followers of **Islam**, called **Muslims**.

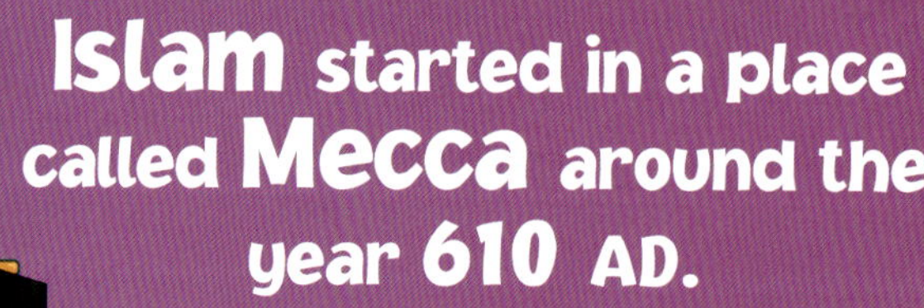

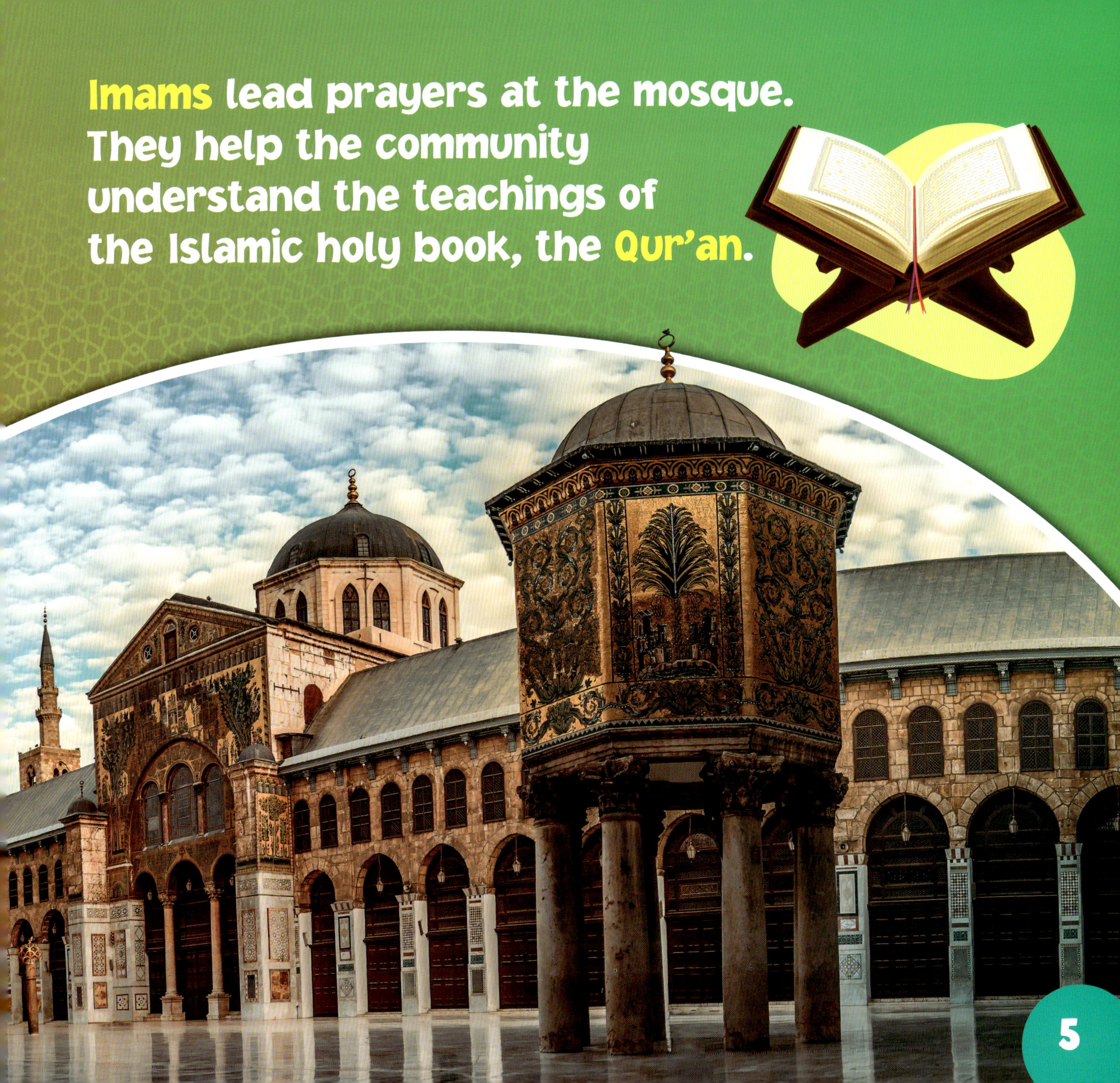

Imams lead prayers at the mosque. They help the community understand the teachings of the Islamic holy book, the Qur'an.

Welcome to the Mosque

There are mosques all around the **world**. The way they look depends on where they are.

The towers on a mosque are called **minarets**. The minarets can be used to call the **Adhan**. This is a call to prayer.

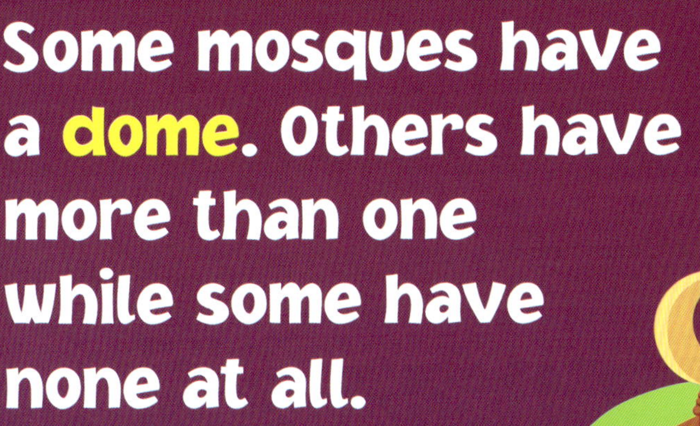

Some mosques have a **dome**. Others have more than one while some have none at all.

Holiest Mosques in the World

Al-Haram Mosque

Mecca, Saudi Arabia

It is built around the Kaaba. This is a shrine Muslims should visit at least once in their life.

Al-Masjid an-Nabawi

Medina, Saudi Arabia

It was built by the prophet Muhammad in 622 AD. Muhammad is the founder of Islam.

Al-Aqsa Mosque

Jerusalem, Israel

According to the Qur'an, Muhammad was taken up to heaven from the site where this mosque is today.

Inside the Mosque

People who enter a mosque must take off their **shoes**. Men and women dress in **loose clothes** that cover their bodies. Many Muslim women cover their hair using a **headscarf**.

The prayer hall has a floor made of **carpet**. Worshipers pray on the floor in lines. Men and women pray in **separate areas** of the mosque.

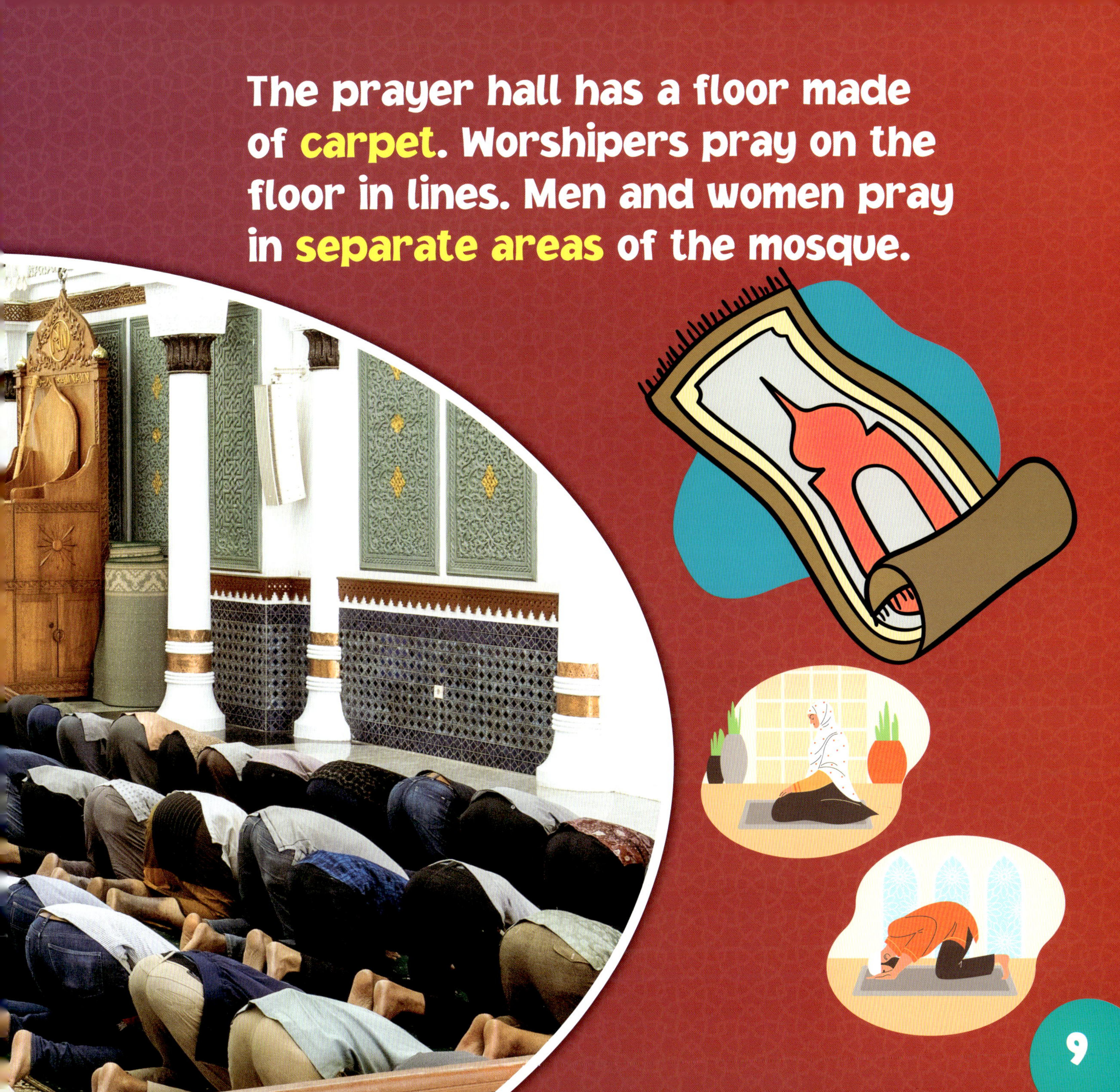

Wudu

Muslims must be clean before they pray. This is called **wudu**.

Some mosques have **fountains** or **taps** outside for people to perform **wudu**.

Wudu involves washing the **hands** three times, as well as the **mouth**, **nose**, **face**, **lower arms**, and **feet**. This makes sure that a person is clean and ready for prayers.

Minbar

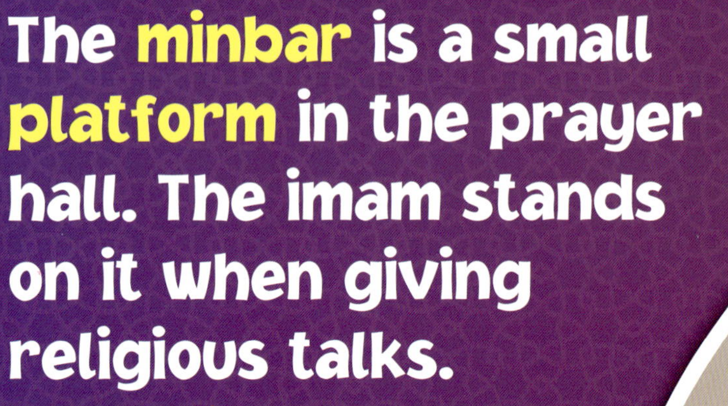

The **minbar** is a small **platform** in the prayer hall. The imam stands on it when giving religious talks.

There are no pictures or statues in the prayer hall. Instead, there are usually **patterns** on its **ceilings** and **walls**.

Mihrab

The **mihrab** is usually next to the minbar. The mihrab is a decorated part of the wall. It marks the direction that Muslims must face when they pray.

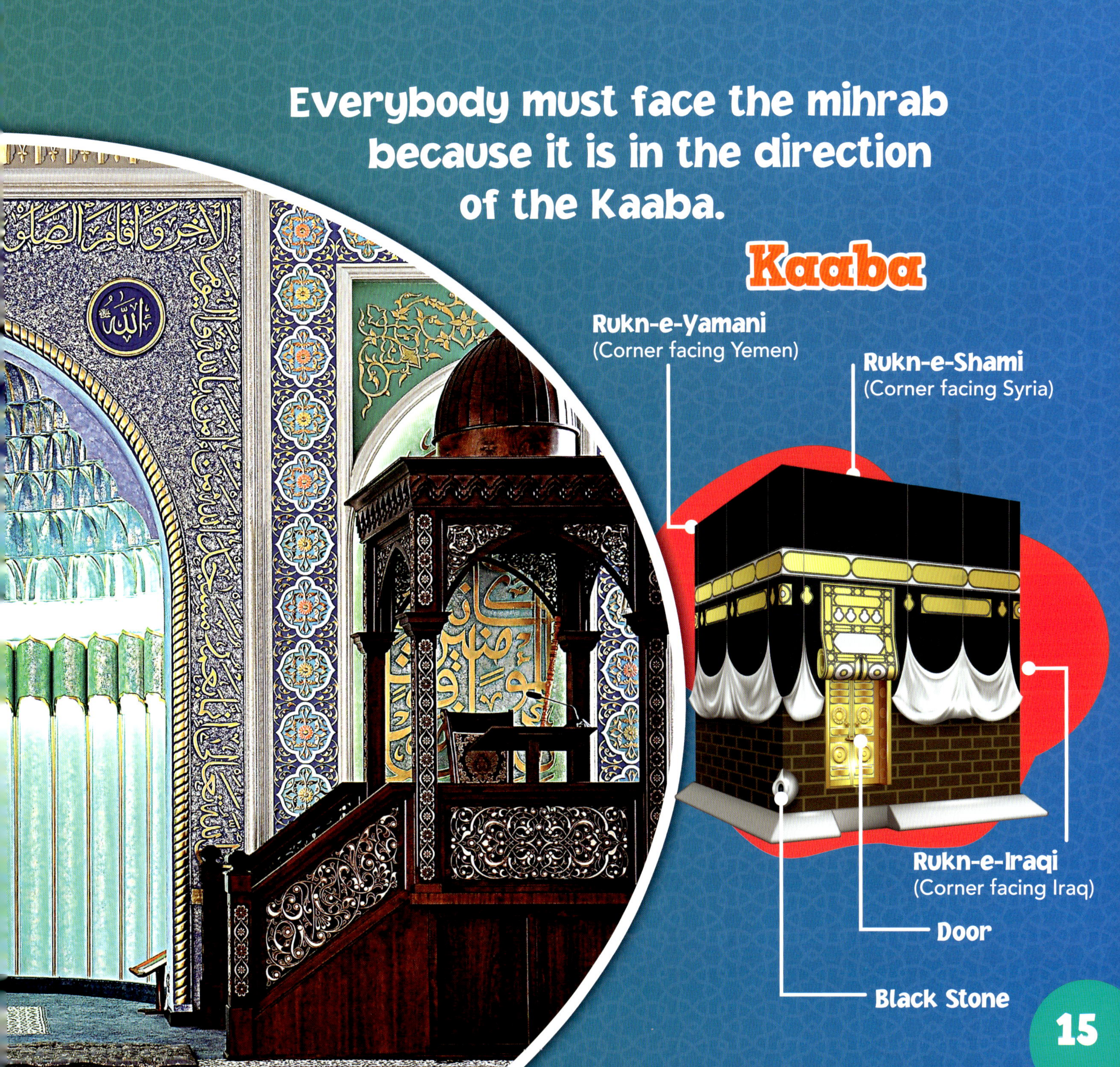
Everybody must face the mihrab because it is in the direction of the Kaaba.
Kaaba
Rukn-e-Yamani
(Corner facing Yemen)
Rukn-e-Shami
(Corner facing Syria)
Rukn-e-Iraqi
(Corner facing Iraq)
Door
Black Stone

Praying

Salat means "prayer." Muslims must perform salat five times a day. Salat is one of the five **pillars** of Islam.

During prayers, people say lines from the Qur'an. **Bowing** and doing the **prostration** position are also part of daily salat.

Daily Prayers

Fajr
The prayer before sunrise

Dhuhr
The prayer after the Sun reaches the highest point in the sky

Asr
The prayer in the late afternoon

Maghrib
The prayer after sunset

Isha
The prayer in the night

Salat al-Jummah

Not everyone is able to visit the mosque each day to pray. Salat al-Jummah is held at the mosque every Friday. It is usually held at the time of the Dhuhr prayer.

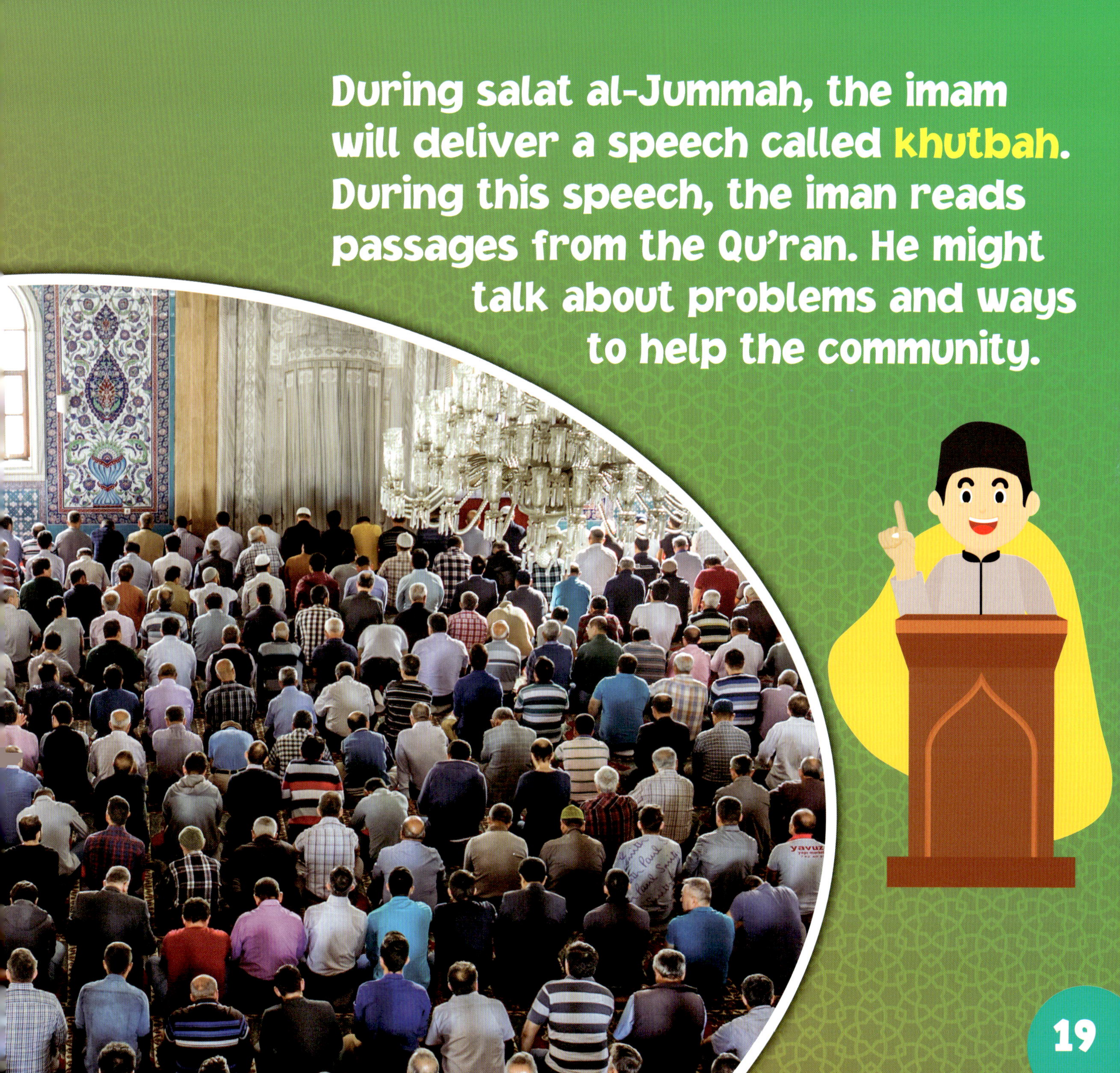

During salat al-Jummah, the imam will deliver a speech called **khutbah**. During this speech, the iman reads passages from the Qu'ran. He might talk about problems and ways to help the community.

Eid al-Fitr and Eid al-Adha

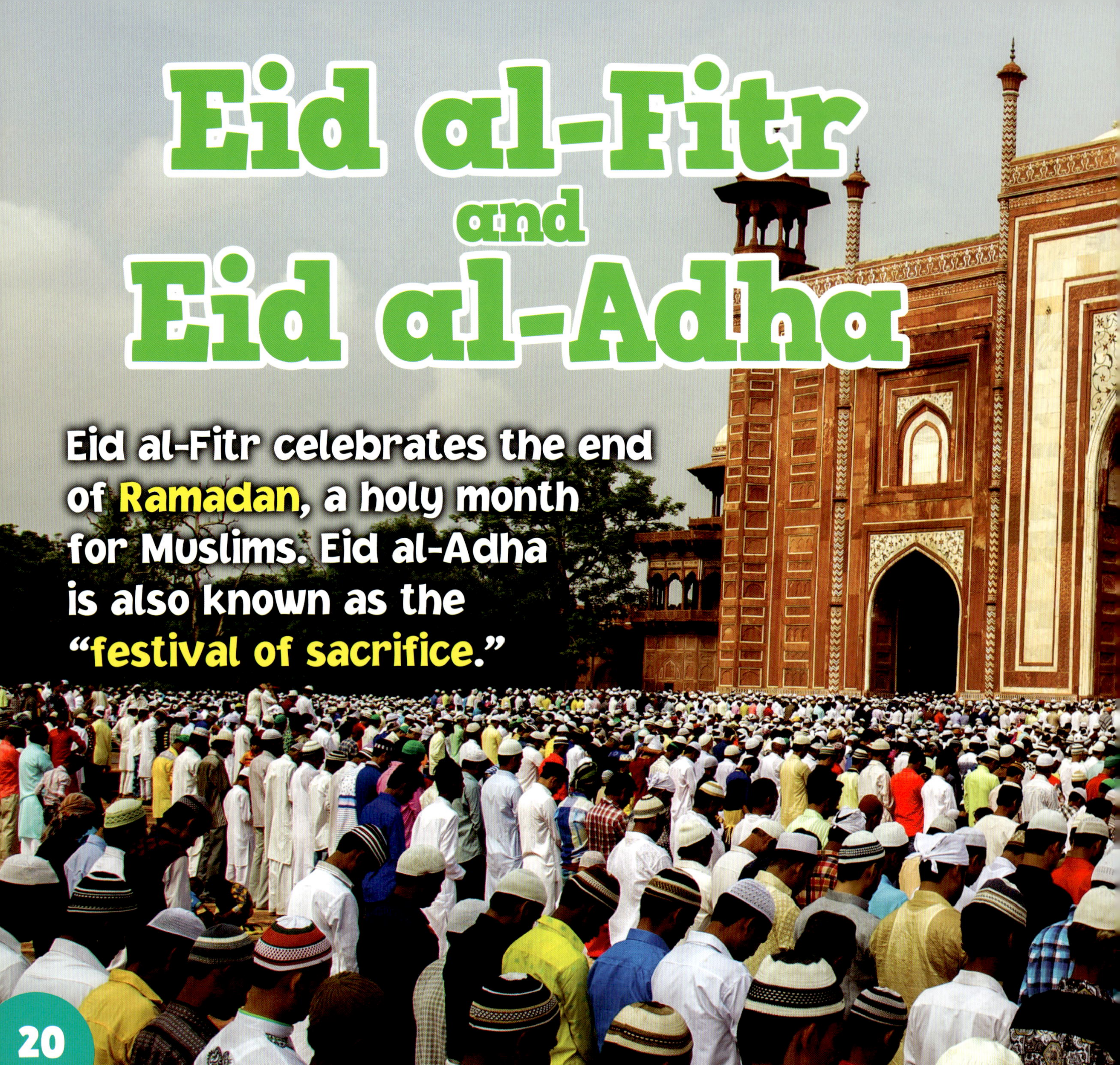

Eid al-Fitr celebrates the end of **Ramadan**, a holy month for Muslims. Eid al-Adha is also known as the "**festival of sacrifice.**"

Everybody gathers at the mosque for **salat al-eid**, or eid prayers. Imams usually give a special khutbah at the end of the service.

During the sacred month of **Ramadan**, Muslims fast from **dawn** until **sunset**.

Mosques around the World

Shah Mosque
Isfahan, Iran

Islamic Center
Washington, DC,
United States

Great Mosque
Kairouan, Tunisia
Sultan Ahmet
Camii Mosque
Istanbul, Türkiye

KEY WORDS

Research has shown that as much as 65 percent of all written material published in English is made up of 300 words. These 300 words cannot be taught using pictures or learned by sounding them out. They must be recognized by sight. This book contains 97 common sight words to help young readers improve their reading fluency and comprehension. This book also teaches young readers several important content words, such as proper nouns.

Page	Sight Words First Appearance
4	a, around, been, for, have, in, is, me, of, place, started, the, to, with, year, you
5	at, book, help, they
6	all, are, be, call, can, look, on, there, this, way, where, world
7	and, by, from, it, life, more, once, one, others, should, some, than, their, up, was, while
8	many, men, must, off, people, take, that, who
9	has, lines, made
10	before, or
11	as, face, feet, hands, makes, three, times, well
12	small, talks, when
13	its, no, pictures
14	next, part
15	because
16	also, day, means, say
17	after, late, night, point
18	each, every, not
19	about, he, might, reads, will
20	end
21	give, until

Page	Content Words First Appearance
4	building, followers, Islam, Mecca, mosque, Muslims, worship
5	community, imams, prayers, Qur'an, teachings
6	Adhan, minarets, towers
7	Al-Aqsa Mosque, Al-Haram Mosque, Al-Masjid an-Nabawi, dome, founder, heaven, Israel, Jerusalem, Kaaba, Medina, Muhammad, prophet, Saudi Arabia, shrine, site
8	bodies, clothes, hair, headscarf, shoes, women
9	areas, carpet, floor, hall, worshipers
10	fountains, taps, wudu
11	arms, mouth, nose, person
12	minbar, platform
13	ceilings, patterns, statues, walls
14	direction, mihrab
15	black stone, corner, door, Rukn-e-Iraqi, Rukn-e-Shami, Rukn-e-Yemani
16	pillars, position, prostration, salat
17	afternoon, Asr, Dhuhr, Fajr, Isha, maghrib, sky, Sun, sunrise, sunset
18	Friday, salat-al-Jummah
19	khutbah, passages, problems, speech
20	Eid al-Adha, Eid al-Fitr, festival, month, Ramadan, sacrifice
21	dawn, salat-el-eid, service

Published by Lightbox Learning Inc.
276 5th Avenue, Suite 704 #917
New York, NY 10001
Website: www.openlightbox.com

Library of Congress Control Number: 2024935531

ISBN 978-1-5105-8193-7 (hardcover)
ISBN 979-8-8745-1512-6 (softcover)
ISBN 978-1-5105-8194-4 (static multi-user eBook)
ISBN 978-1-5105-8196-8 (interactive multi-user eBook)

Printed in Guangzhou, China
1 2 3 4 5 6 7 8 9 0 28 27 26 25 24

052024
100923

Project Coordinator: Sara Cucini
Designer: Jean Faye Rodriguez

Every reasonable effort has been made to trace ownership and to obtain permission to reprint copyright material. The publisher would be pleased to have any errors or omissions brought to its attention so that they may be corrected in subsequent printings.

The publisher acknowledges Getty Images, Alamy, and Shutterstock as the primary image suppliers for this title.

First published by BookLife in 2020.